Diviner

Diviner

Eugene O'Connell

Three Spires Press

First published in 2009
by
Three Spires Press
11-12 St Stephen's Street,
Off Tower Street,
Cork,
Ireland.

threespirespress@gmail.com

Copyright © Eugene O'Connell 2009

The moral rights of the author have been asserted.

ISBN 978-1-873548-52-3
(paperback)
ISBN 978-1-873548-53-0
(hardback edition limited to one hundred numbered and signed)

The author and publisher gratefully acknowledge a grant from
Cork County Council (Arts Department)
towards the publication of this book.

Printed by the MPG Books Group in the UK

You fellows, come and be on hand,
We're headed for Scluraffen land
And yet we're stuck in mud and sand.

– Narrenschiff

Contents

Curtain Call 13
Hors d'oeuvre 14
Mamma Mia 15
Seeing the Light 16
Mon Amour 17
The Keener 18
Misprision 19
Ostpolitik 20
Negative Equity 21
Off Cuts 22
The Midwife's Tale 23
Plain Chant 25
On the Pier 26
Apron Strings 27
A la Carte 28
The Rounded Life 29
Mirror Mirror 30
Angst 31
Hob Orator 32
Loaves and Fishes 33
Quack 34
Oracle 35
Gombeen 36
In Hock 37

Of Golden Calves 38
Of Boors 39
Nuisance Call 40
Memento Mori 41
Chinese Box 42
Redundant Bell Ringer 43
Decorum 44
Diviner 45
Boodle 46
The Churl's Tale 47
The Two Days 49
Janus 51
Death of a Poet 52
Cuirt 53
Abbeyfeale: A Directory 54
The Girl at Information 56
Coquette 57
Doubting Thomas 58
Volte Face 59
Inamorata 60
White Christmas, Kiskeam, '07 61
Coda 62
Anam 63
Pieta 64

Acknowledgments

I would like to thank the editors of the following periodicals where some of these poems or versions of them have appeared,

The Temenos Academy Review; The Stony Thursday Book; Southword; Agenda; Cork Review; Cork Literary Review; The Shop; Poetry Ireland Review; Strands; Seanchas Duthalla; Sliabh Luachra Magazine; The Stinging Fly.

A special word of thanks to Ian McDonagh, Arts Officer (Cork County Council) for a bursary towards the publication of this book.

Note: the epigraphs to the sonnet sequence 'The Rounded Life' are from the German of Sebastian Brant's *Narrenschiff* or *Ship of Fools* (c.1492). The English texts are my own versions based on the literal translations of Edwin H. Zeydel.

Curtain Call

Words were drawn to you, Mother,
Though you were hard of hearing.
Words from the telly in the corner
When the characters talked loud.
Words from papers you'd cut pieces
Out of and tucked under you, newspaper
Columns that lifted you to our level.
Though you were as small as a child
When you stood at the arm of the chair
Looking beyond us at a place you'd reach
Before we'd wake, surprising us…
As if an actor waiting in the wing
Would miss a cue, once the curtain
Was pulled and the lights went down.

Hors d'oeuvre

Pushing ninety you've developed
A taste for earth, a fetish for seed
You put in whatever pot or pan
Is near at hand and doesn't cost.
So the house is littered with limbs
Of plants sporting wrist tags,
Like babies in an incubator or
Soldiers going off to the war.
High maintenance divas propped
In prime spots on the window sill
Demanding delicacies – caked cow-shit
For hors d'oeuvre if you don't mind.
Beware of earth, Mother, a thankless
Taskmaster who won't return the favour.

Mamma Mia

after Brian Patten

She reeks of death, doesn't she?
I look at the sky and ask,
No it said no,
She'll do as I do, I go on,
She'll go on forever.

She reeks of death, doesn't she?
I look at the earth and ask,
No it said no,
She'll do as I do, I go on,
She'll go on forever.

She reeks of death, doesn't she?
I look at the fire and ask,
No it said no,
She'll do as I do, I go on,
She'll go on forever.

She reeks of death, doesn't she?
I look at the river and ask,
No it said no,
She'll do as I do, I go on,
She'll go on forever.

She reeks of death, doesn't she?
I look her in the eye and ask,
No she said no,
She'll do as I do, I go on,
She'll go on forever.

Seeing the Light

After she draws the pension on Friday
I drive my mother to the graveyard,
She walks among the dead and prays
While I read the newspaper in the car.
I envy how near she is to them, how
Soon she will join the dear departed.
I was in love like that once, consumed
By the idea of 'love' until I realised that
It's not all that people make it out to be.
I envy your faith Mama, your prayer book
Bulging with photographs of the missing,
Your trust in that ghostly other-world
More real to you than the one
You see every day with your eyes.

Mon Amour

Something that catches my eye
Out the car window makes me
Pull in to the beach at Inch,
To look out over the waves
At Tír Na nÓg, the land of youth
Níamh and Oisín left for on a ghost
Horse who came in over the water.
Turning to where you would have been
At my shoulder I wonder if you've
Left for that Isle, found your Prince –
An Über-god in shining armour or
Feet of clay, like the one at the wheel
Of a blue Corolla parked so it can see
Out over the heaving ocean's mane.

The Keener

Nora Singleton lost the run of herself
After her husband died in a horse fall,
Turning up unannounced at the funeral
Of a complete stranger she'd cradle
The head of the corpse in her breast,
Launch into this lament that people had
Forgotten until it came alive in her mouth.
The story of a woman putting her lips
To her dying husband's wound and drinking
Before the blood flowed on to the ground.
So vivid a tale that people could imagine
Themselves being there, being astounded
At the words coming out of the mouth
Of the woman with the wine red lips.

Misprision

for Nuala Fenton

'*Irene, goodnight Irene*
I'll see you in my dreams'

I'm drawn to the man with his ear
To the donkey's head at the Fenton,
I'm trying to imagine what the donkey
Is saying that has the man as engrossed
As Bernadette at the sight of Our Lady.
There's no catalogue going with the piece
So I ask the girl at the desk who thinks
"'The thing' is not on exhibition at all,
Only that Irene er Miss Fenton didn't get
'Round to movin' it out to the back yet."
My hunch is that the 'thing' is Miss Fenton's
Little indulgence (lucky donkey) the space
Where she can chill out after the strain
Of the Cooke and Le Brocquoy openings.

Ostpolitik

after the 9th C. Irish

Deirdre put her eye on Naoise
A young fellow of her own age
Who let on to be immune to her charms.
'Heifers pine where there's no bull', she said.
'You have the mother of all bulls at home,' he said,
Meaning Laoghaire, the elder, she was promised to.
'I'd go for the strapping lad if I had choice,'
She said, eyeing the full length of him.
'No can do,' said Naoise, quoting something
From Cathbad the shaman of his own tribe.
Miffed at the lame excuse, she caught him
By the ears and lifted him off the ground.
'Unless you want to be an earless mute
The talk of the western world, you'll marry me.'
'Right so,' he said, once the colour drained
Back into the ashen lobes.

Negative Equity

Because you've built a house
On a hill that can be seen for
Miles around by people who
Look at you coyly and ask
If you're bringing in a wife,
Filling the rooms you'd sub-
Consciously painted pink, brown.
Because you over-saw the build
Made sure the footings were solid,
Doesn't mean you haven't built
On shifting sands, that some time
Traveller pushing through under-
Growth won't find himself framed
In your rubble strewn doorway.

Off Cuts

for Dennis O Connor

Dennis fusses over a dresser
He's making on a bench, the way
A woman fusses over a cake,
A plain piece to store pictures,
Knick knacks from travelled places.
A dresser he'll point at, say things
He thought out before the boom,
When words like dowel, spokeshave,
Were in fashion, and a hand plane
Was taken to anything showy.

Except for the end he'd set down
On the piece of timber, his spirit level
Was plain and spattered, the bubble
Barely showing in the chamber.
He'd close one eye and sight
The beam for confirmation rather
Than reach for what he called
The 'untity', a newly bought level
(Pristine in its plastic wrapping)
That would give him an instant read.

Uninhibited, he'd stand before the job
For a long time without speaking,
Unlike me, who'd have to butt in
With a word or more to fill the silence.
'The holy all of it' to paraphrase his
Own way of talking, was that he was
As hooked on his trade as I'm on mine,
Except that his box of 'fol dols' had
A tool for every job under the sun,
While I have only the pen and paper.

The Midwife's Tale

Aileen had settled herself in a bed in the corner of her cabin and was about to go to sleep when she heard a knock on the door. Being an obliging woman she opened it to a tall dark stranger who asked if she would help his wife who was about to give birth.

In the twinkle of an eye Aileen found herself lifted on to the back of a horse who galloped over fields until they reached the bank of a river. 'God and the Virgin between us and all harm,' she exclaimed as they plunged into the water.

'Say those words again at your peril,' growled the man in front of her in the saddle, though his mood softened when they reached a large green mound. One stamp of his foot and a door opened to a great underground feast, ladies and gentlemen dancing.

Led by an unseen hand Aileen found herself in a room where a beautiful woman was giving birth to a baby boy. An ointment was procured from the father, as was the custom of the time, to rub on to the baby's body, though he warned her not to rub the ointment on to any part of her own skin.

Aileen felt an itch in her eye and accidentally rubbed some of the ointment into it. Something strange happened, she could see the reality behind the show of things out of the eye that she had rubbed and ordinary life out of the other one. The beautiful woman became a withered old hag, the baby a bawling brat and the tall handsome stranger a sneering dwarf.

Home after her experience Aileen fell into a deep sleep and woke the next morning wondering if she had dreamed the strange happenings of the night before. It being a Fair Day in the nearby town she gathered her basket of eggs and odds and ends and went to it.

She was surprised to see the tall dark stranger at the fair before her, when she closed one eye and looked at him again, she could see him as he really was.

She followed at a distance and saw him chat up an innocent country girl who was about to go off with him when Aileen exclaimed in a loud voice: 'God and the Virgin between us and all harm.'

The stranger turned on Aileen, plunged his stick into the eye that she could see the truth out of and disappeared forever.

Plain Chant

Begging your pardon Father, but I'd prefer
To have him in Marbella, pink champagne
By the pool, bouquets of Bougonvaille,
Than him wasting away there in a box.
Begging your pardon Father, but I'd prefer
If you didn't have to read the words out
Of the Book over him, promises, promises.
I'd prefer to have him in Marbella, bouquets
Of Bougonvillae rather than spur of the moment
Roses plucked out of a tub at Spar.
Begging your pardon Father, but I'd prefer
To have him in Marbella, pink champagne
By the pool, bouquets of Bougonvaille,
Wolf whistles at my little black number.

On the Pier

The yellow of a lake in Autumn
Washes my eyes, clarifies.
A breeze blows open the pages
Of the album you gave me.
Time passes so I'm not sure
If it was your eyes hair or mouth
That had the peculiar colour of smoke.
Sorrow is a mood: the lake lifts,
The geese with undercarriage down
Coming in to land, the sound
Of a flute carrying over the water .

Apron Strings

after Gregory O Donoghue

Guilty as charged, I turned
My mother into a Madonna,
Do this, do that, drudge, drudge,
Yet when I take out a pen to rhyme
Or don new duds (in case I fall
Under a bus or meet Miss Right)
She frowns and I go out
Full of pity at that look.
Poets who turn their mothers
Into plaster saints deserve nothing
Better than to be burned on a pyre
Of their own unpublished verse,
Their ashes dumped instead of
Floated in a ghat on whatever
Local river passes for the Ganges.

Á la Carte

for my mother

Fussing if we came in hungry
Outside the appointed meal-time
She'd come up somehow with
A plate of bacon and cabbage,
More common or garden fare
Than the loaves and fishes
Conjured by the chef at Galilee.

The Rounded Life

for James Harpur

Who measures heaven earth and sea
Thus seeking lore or gaiety
Let him beware a fool to be.

Wise old number cruncher Archimedes
Would sit on the beach at Syracuse
Drawing lines and angles in the sand,
Knowing that the sea would roll in and
Wipe out his day's work, he'd start again.
Walking the shore-line to clear his head
He's pick whatever debris caught his eye,
Bits of flotsam, bric a brac, enough to make
A mandala, the picture flower people spread
On the pavement of a busy shopping mall
That shoppers curse under their breath,
Yet tiptoe round, proving his hypothesis
That the heart rules rather than the head,
Will not allow beauty to be disturbed.

Mirror, Mirror

My time in fool's broth I must pass
Since I esteem the looking glass
I'm brother to a silly ass.

Which of us, hand on heart, can swear
He passed a mirror without looking
At his own reflection, not realising that
Others see a dunce's cap on the head
That's fussed over as if it was Cleopatra's.
A head he'd swear on the holy book is
Wiser more debonair, as fit to hold office
As any high court Judge or Taoiseach.
Besotted with himself this dunce forgets
The story of Narcissus the boy who fell
In love with his own reflection in a well.
The gold washed out of his hair when
He was found, the colours of the Adonis
As withered as a handful of old grass.

Angst

Who lights his lamp here, warm and bright
And lets the oil give cheering light
That man shall ever give delight.

Believe it or not, there are creatures
Of the earth that we can learn from,
The locust who'll swarm once he feels
A hunger pang regardless of what 'copter
Spray or bongo-beaters range against him.
The spider who'll hang his web wherever
He can hook a line, won't worry if his
Postal code is Mount Merrion or Soweto.
Creatures of the earth with purpose
While we fantasise, if only, if only.
Since no one has mapped out wherever
It is we're going and come back to tell us,
Why should we fret? Worry feeds on worry,
Will a fire tell whoever is feeding it to stop.

Hob Orator

If all men's cares you fain would borrow
And you neglect your joy and sorrow
You'll get a fool's broth on the morrow

A melted fool, an amadán, the man
Who'd take on more than his own
Fair share of the worries of the world.
Not content until the bones of his face
Poke through his skin, pucker the baby
Faced good looks he was born with.
Should take a leaf out of the book
Of Diogenes, a wise man of the ancient
World who lived in a tub, was confident
Enough to tell the emperor Alexander
(Who stopped to talk to him on the way
To war) to move out of the light of the sun
'A greater king than he,' or come to think of it,
Than the hob orator himself in the barrel.

Loaves and Fishes

Who says; no pity God avows,
And that no justice He doth house,
Is ignorant as geese and sows.

Once called, the local man
Went to the river to fish
For a trout that he cooked
And eat out of a frying pan.
Did himself up and walked
Over to the village to meet
The other fellas' in the pub.
'Broke bread', as he put it.
Walks home and is found
With the smoking barrel
Of a shotgun in his hand.
His face set around a note
He made for himself alone
Before he blew it into the sky.

Quack

The medico who'd treat and cure
But of his skill is never sure
The man's an idiot simon pure.

Though you doubted that Reidy
The local medicine man would
Do any more for you than the piss
Testing and rolling round in a tunnel
The hospital doctors put you through,
You'd still go along, hoping there
Was more to his talk than bluster –
That there might be something
In the 'bottle' he had in the coat –
That the tumour grown big as a ball
In your belly might shrink, bit by bit
Day by day, until the pin in the clasp
Of the belt around your waist fitted
Into the old well worn groove.

Oracle

The world is full of superstition
Men prophesy by stars position
And every fool deems this his mission

Oul' Moore was a non de plume for the author
Of a farm diary, the well thumbed Bible
Of the fifties house-hold that I grew up in.
Lists of Marts and Fair Days played second fiddle
To the horoscopes – an afterthought of the publisher
Most likely, that grew legs, were talked of in the
Same breath as the prophecies of Nostradamus.
The shock when we came of age and were big
Enough to reach up to the shelf to discover that
The much hyped Almanac was no more than a farm
Year book with lists of cow and horse sales was on
A par with the discovery that Santa was a fraud, or
That we could go to the beach at Ballybunion more
Than the one prescribed day in September.

Gombeen

Who weds and for naught else is fain
Than growth of property and gain
Will suffer quarrels woe and pain.

Be honest, would you trust a man
Who'd sell his youthful years for gain,
Because you like the smell of fat
Why skin your donkey just for that.

Who weds an auld wan just for dough
Makes one grand splurge then oh no,
Because you like the smell of fat
Why skin your donkey just for that.

No out clause in his pre-nup contract
'Your 'man' is beggared if he default,
Because you like the smell of fat
Why skin your donkey just for that.

Nothing in his life but woe, Bog Latin,
With his 'God incrase' ye sir an' gratis.'

In Hock

Who in his borrowing's too free
The payment date the wolf will see
Meanwhile the ass will kick his knee

The man who's cagey when he borrows
Has few cares and fewer sorrows,
Trust not the man he is not true
Who's affable and lends to you.
He'll bleed you dry if you don't pay
Strip your roof let in the sky,
Ms. Wolf his bit of glam will come
To claim her pound of flesh and bone.
Your belongings in a bag you'll go
To live at Simon with the low…
Hobo, Hobo, you'll hear the chant that
Reminds you of the old school rhyme.
'When donkeys want to dance don't fail
To give them room don't hold their tail.'

Of Golden Calves

Vile scolding words do irritate
Good manners thereby will abate
If sow-bells rung from morn to late.

Maybe it's my age, correct me if I'm wrong,
But is the world teeming with morons,
Cock of the walk on stages mouthing
Mumbo-jumbo to houses full of dunces.
Idols foaming at the mouth, teasing until
The people in a frenzy call for more, more,
As if this painted doxie, this Jezebel
Would somehow satisfy their craving,
This bloated Idol that lambastes what's
Left of sober sense, good taste.
Feted in the papers of the world, her ass
More familiar to the public than her face.
Fool holds the sow's ear, wags her head,
Oul' dacency's gone out of fashion, dated.

Of Boors

Some think their wit is very fine
But they are geese right down the line
All reason, breeding they decline.

There's one in every street, the one
You have to tiptoe round, the boor
There's no talking to, drives an S.U.V.
A guzzler with a hand free mobile so
He's free to give the fingers in traffic.
Tiff with the wife, he's at the local
Drowning his sorrows, what's worse he's
Bright enough to see the error of his way
Yet refuses to repent. Elephant in the room
Who should be brought to book at once
Instead of being humoured, untold
The damage that's done in the name of
A 'bit of quiet', when what's needed is
Old fashioned gumption, confrontation.

Nuisance Call

> The man who would on truth insist
> Must meet this, that antagonist
> Who'll try and force him to desist.

A gentleman to his fingertips,
Won't mind if you buttonhole
Him on a matter that has been
Of concern to you of late.
Will refer you to, 'a man up the line'
Who has your contact details and
Will get back to you, 'rest assured'.
A conscientious fellow who'll ring
You when you're number's up in lights
On his cell-phone, a mover and shaker
(Believe you me) who won't let up
Until you drop whatever you are doing
At that precise nano-second in time,
Lift the receiver from its cradle.

Memento Mori

The longest memory in my head
Is the day Breda Leary was called
Out of Mrs. Vaughan's fifth year
Geography class in Boherbue,
Her face the colour of puce
With what she heard although
It was May and the season
Was about to bloom; her pencil
(The one with the chewed top)
Sprawled across the Black Sea
On the page of the atlas still
Open on her desk, like a shovel
Thrown across the mouth
Of an open grave.

Chinese Box

in memory of Micheal Davitt

I pulled at the ribbon
Of the box they said
You left me, pulled
At the ribbon of the box
Inside that and so on
Ad infinitum,
Until it dawned on me
That there was no Present,
No ribbon to pull once
The magician had disappeared
Into a box that can only
Be opened from the inside.

Redundant Bell Ringer

after Daibhí O Brúadair

More fool than the half-wit
This new bell would make of me,
This excuse for an angelus
Croaking morning noon and night.

Pity I can't mimic the stutter
Of this imported alien, this belching
Chip that has as much music
In it as a public house fart.

I'd take a man if there is one
In this god-forsaken village,
Wrap myself round him in public
Set their tongues wagging,

Who have more respect for SUV's
Than the seasoned hand of a bell ringer,
O if what I spent on pulling an auld rope
I'd spent on a fancy man and style.

Decorum

Regular's at Johnie D's public house
Were so used to the sight of Jack Titus
Dancing around the floor with a drink
Of Guinness above his head, calling
Lishin to Pata Lishin to Pata
That none of them would take a blind
Bit of notice, but would be offended
At blow-ins to the area who looked
For longer than was appropriate at the
Spectacle of a grown man in overcoat
And dung encrusted hob nailed boots,
Shuffling around the pub floor muttering
To himself, a wound-up ballerina with
A glass of Stout in an up stretched hand.

Diviner

For Dan Bat

Who would walk the land
With a rod that trembled
In his hand when he found
Spring wells he could drain.

Who would prod the fields
With the tooth of a skeeter
Holing the pan under the earth
So water drained into its bowels.

Who stopped when his hips gave
His body fell and he saw the world
Again as a child, ear to the ground,
Listening to the sound of water.

Boodle

after Eogan Rúa O Súilleabhain

Séamus, auld stock of the block, blood brother
Will you make me a handle of a spade
And a foot piece to go with it, knowing you
It will be as elegant a tool as broke earth.

A weapon that will deal with praties quicker
Than any spailpín from here to Mayo, so willing
It will be all I can do to keep up, so supple
I need only break sweat to collect my pay.

If the Gaffer is slow to cough up, I'll put on
Airs, bamboozle the óinseach with stories
Of Helen's trouble at Troy, of Caesar's
Predicament at the Rubicon river.

I'll hoard every cent while the digging lasts
In a purse tied to my vest and sown until
We meet up at Young Dan's in Clamper,
Plank our elbows on the counter and call

For porter, for whiskey for the house, for
Friend and foe until the boodle's gone,
There will be no pockets in the coat
I'll be wearing when the talk is done.

The Churl's Tale

Jack was a sour distant man who rarely allowed a smile to crease his face, though he had regular features that brought him a wife and children. A man who steered clear of any dealings with the 'other world' until one night on the way home from the pub he heard a person moaning on the side of the road.

Jack put the feeble old body into his cart, plied it with whiskey and put it in a warm bed. Woken in the morning by a strange unearthly light the 'Samaritan' found himself looking at an angel. 'You picked me off the road last night and saved my life so I'm obliged to offer you three wishes.'

Jack rubbed his chin and asked, 'that whoever pulled a branch off his ash tree be glued to it, that whoever sat in his arm-chair be glued to it and that whoever put his hand into the drawer where he kept his things would be glued to it'. The Angel raised his eyebrows at the wishes that he was obliged to grant, adding a codicil that the countryman's narrow-minded attitude bared him from going into heaven.

One evening many years later as Jack sat in his chair thinking about his farm and wife and children, a smell of sulphur came to his nose and a black stranger with horns in his head and hooves on his feet appeared saying 'that as Jack was banned from going into heaven, that a place was prepared for him in the place below if he'd like to come along'.

Rubbing his chin for a minute the countryman got up out of the chair and offered it to the visitor, the Devil was immediately glued to it. Jack set about him with a cudgel and only stopped when the demon swore that he'd never darken his door again.

Soon after another messenger from the 'other world' arrived with instructions to avoid the chair and the countryman's cudgel. Asked if he would like to rest himself in the chair the visitor refused and Jack said 'that he would be going so' if the devil would hand him an awl from the drawer to mend his shoes for the journey. The hand stuck and Jack delivered the mother of all beatings to the unfortunate ogre.

Satan himself got wind of the Churl who refused to take up the place he had specifically made up for him.

Rapping on the door he demanded that the countryman come out, ' I'll go wherever you want but the road is slippery after the ice and I'll need a stick, if I fall and break a leg I wouldn't want your princely shoulders to be carrying my mortal carcase'.

Satan reached for a stick off the Sycamore tree and was immediately glued to it, the Churl set about him for a whole day and a night until he swore an oath that he would never darken the door of Jack's house again.

Barred from heaven and from hell Jack's demeanour lightened, he came out of himself more, played cards and drank into the late hours-now that he was released of any obligations to this world or the hereafter.

The Two Days

in memory of. my father

1.   *Spring*

Racing for after hours in a pub
The Morris broke the width
Of itself in the bridge at Nohoval,
Landed upside down so the driver
Had to climb out a side window,
Dodge a bull standing in the river,
A complication that added
To the glamour of the pub talk.

The story behind the story was
A mute homecoming, a house-woken
To a man whose jaw was set in netting,
A wife going out with a lamp
To inspect the remains of their once
Gleaming wedding morning car.

2 *Fall*

The people of the locality
Knew the sound of his car,
'Read the time', by the noise
Of the engine labouring
Up the Veins, the last hill
Before the run in to Boher.

Talked among themselves
About the hours he idled,
Noticed him wrong footed
By the sun that had moved
In the sky since he went in
To the pub that morning.

Knew that once home he'd go in
To the house before the Volks
Had time to settle, before the oils
Seeping into the sump, plip, plop,
Sounded so loud you'd think that
The quiet had never been disturbed.

Janus
after Guntars Godiņš

Perhaps this river pool,
Perhaps that stretch of horizon,
Perhaps the lens of your glasses
On the mantelpiece in the kitchen,
Who knows where to look for you, Mother?
(Not in the graveyard that will
Moss over your name and birth date,
'A penny for your thoughts
Out there in that distant shore)
Nothing was usual about your life
You married the poet Pludonis,
Who left you with a looking glass
In one hand and the wing
Of a white bird in the other,
'There were many books and much dust,'
You'd say to who ever was in your hearing.

Death of a Poet

Apollinaire died at six
O'clock in the evening
A clock was stopped
At the exact time and
Turned to face the wall,
Out of sync with the custom
Digital time pieces in the house
Ticked on as if to prove
To acolytes who came to
Drink a toast to his life,
That time had its Apollinaire.

Cúirt

for Gerard Smyth

Stuff the fancy dans, the preening
Word queens of Connemara,
Step out into the horde of people
Descended upon the city of the tribes.
Snap: ducks in a dried up dock,
Martins playing molly bawn with flies
Over the heads of the wildly swinging
Fishermen in the quicksilver Corrib.
Stuff the fancy dans, the preening
Word queens of Connemara,
Step out into the unwashed horde,
Snap the wonderfully inappropriate
Icon of the Madonna and Child
In the cathedral of the playboy bishop.

Abbeyfeale: A Directory

for John McAuliffe

'by his death religion lost a shining light,
the cause of temperance a strenuous advocate'

(from the Fr Casey statue)

    For hospitality. See Leen's Hotel on the Main Street. See Thade Lynch's Ramble Inn 'out the Ballybunion Road'. See D.J.Murphy's Select Bar, see inscription on front wall that reads, 'seven reasons for drinking Guinness (Strength, Nerves, Digestion, Exhaustion, Sleeplessness, Tonic for the blood)'.

    For food. See Mo's Oriental Thai and Chinese. See Superma's burger and chips New Street. See Daly's near the AIB 'new treats include Dressed Crab, King Prawns in butter'. See Little Nero's at the monument. See Toors for an Indian. See the Orchid next to the newly opened Adrenalin Rush – one stop motor cycle shop.

    For Diversion. See CJ's Flix and Mix video emporium. See Spin City Luna Park Carnival 'in the town park until Sept. 7th'. See the Deep End Nite Club. See The Last King of Scotland – bio pic of Idi Amin showing at the Abbey 'a heart thumping thriller'. See Lal Browne or Ladbrokes for the Gi Gi's.

    For a makeover. See Billy Mann's Gents Hairdresser or Ya Man (same proprietor). See Martina Keane Stryker's Golden Scissors at the Athea end of Main Street' also offers ear piercing'. See Fuschia Hair and Beauty Studio. See Norma's at the junction of New Street and Main 'the new ghl styler…thou shalt never be the same girl twice'.

For the arts and history. See Jack Foleys live music every weekend. See Matt McCoy's (DJ Sparky till close). See the Eddie Lee band, see special guest Lena 'great night in store'. See the Fr Casey statue in the square – the bronze forefinger wagging — See Epigraph.

The Girl at Information

The woman behind the counter at Information
At Knock shrine goes on about the smell:
'This pong from her fingers from wonce she's
Got up this morning worse'n fish somethin' rotten'.
Goes on and on while the people in the queue listen:
'A smell the carbolic soap itself even won't shift'.
The eyes of the people in the queue glaze over,
Wonder who'll wheel the blind and the lame
To the gable where the Virgin, Saint Joseph and John
Appeared on a wet night in eighteen seventy nine.
'Gran' babies', according to eleven year old Pat Hill,
One of the fifteen villagers who saw the sight,
'Drawin' back from the hands, God help us,
That'd I'v been scrubbed if we only knew'.

Coquette

in memory of Dennis O Connor

'rock of ages'

Out of deference to the woman
Who stood on a rock looking out
Over his farm of land for as long
As he could remember, he'd peel
The cap from his head, beat his breast
Whenever he passed her by in a car,
Or walking with a bag of messages.
As to whether he noticed (or because
He was 'nature's gentleman' went along
With what the neighbours wanted)
That the face of the woman didn't age
Like the flesh of the others in the parish,
Or didn't lose its composure despite
What she was hearing from the people.

Doubting Thomas

Whoever or whatever, since we might be here
By chance, ordained that we come to life
Also ordained that we grow tired of wonders.
The visionaries at Knock went for supper
Knowing that the vision would not last.
Or the day I myself took a breather from
A once in a lifetime sighting of an otter
Showing itself in a gully miles upstream
From the river where it had been born.
Knowing that the vision would not last
Until I got back, that however I embellished
The story for the sceptic in the pub, nothing
Would compensate for the finger in the wound,
The shock at the eyes in the head of the being.

Volte-Face

for Peter O Connell

They are not long
The days of wine and roses

Tired of the other world Plato decided
To come back to earth as a steel erector,
Learned the language, fell in with a crew.
'A shade more, a shade,' he'd bellow at
The men struggling to lift a pole the final
Fraction so that it could be bolted home.
And being of the other world lived on while
The men around him died one by one,
Dan Mac of the Freeholes, Pa Donnelly.
And wouldn't go back to the Elysian Field
Once he'd remembered the tasteless wine
On his tongue, the jaded conversation
Unlike the banter of the men at Dan Jo's,
The 'blood up' at something someone said.

Inamorata

in memory of Danny Joe

I won't talk to you again or hear your voice
Or see you again brother — dearer than life.
I'll love you forever though, make odes
To celebrate you, as under the apple tree
Procne sang of the fate of his lost Itylis.
I'll send you these lines from Catullus'
Ode to his brother C. Quintilus Martius:
'So you won't think your words are lost in air
Or the thoughtfulness of your nature forgotten.'
The day, for example, in Mount Alvernia hospital
You took us to the apple tree in the grounds
Out back, surfed the windfall until you came up
With an armful of the most glorious Cookers,
'For a tart for Mama', you said, offering the horde.

White Christmas, Kiskeam '07

> ' *I only know what the words know*'
> Samuel Beckett

A red fox comes into view
When I pull back the curtains
Of the window, is mobbed
By a magpie and a small bird,
Isn't deflected from it's course,
Clears the river in one bound
And disappears into the iced-
Over field on the other side.
Pen after pen in Mamas' jam-jar
Is empty when I go to write,
The windows in the envelopes
Breaking the rhythm of my lines,
I'll lift the paper up to the light
To see what the ballpoints said.

Coda

If it is true that we will all meet
After we 'shuffle off this mortal coil',
Wouldn't it be nice to be woken up
By the sound of Maggie the Road's
Cock crowing out over the countryside,
Rather than by the ear splitting din
Of the Archangel Gabriel's trumpet.
Console ourselves with the thought that
We could sleep in while Mother, as usual,
Stoked the fire in the grate, the noise
Of her labour putting the 'doties' at ease.
Until we realised that sooner or later
She would call for us 'to be puttin'
A dock on yer'selves for the road'.

Anam

after Séan O Riordáin

Whatever comes, goes and returns
As our first soul in all it's glory.

And the older man is destined
To do as the child in him ordained.

And realise there is nothing beyond
The substance of the spirit he is given.

Though we lose sight of that now and again
Expecting a change in our essential form.

We come back empty after every journey
To the eternity of our own first self .

Pieta

in memory of Tim Carroll

The best day of the year was when
Tim Carroll came to kill the pig,
His pockets bulging with sticky
Sweet bulls eyes, a treat
For us children while he talked
To the grown ups and drank Stout.

We didn't care about the pig, grown
Huge and reeking in her chamber,
Or close our ears to her screams on
The way to the table, so long as she
Didn't bite or kick us with the leg
We were given to hold.

Lucky it was Teresa's job to hold
The pan for the blood under the throat,
Or we'd have missed seeing the insides.
The heart that was like our own,
The bladder that was blown into
A football for us to kick like

We were Pele in the World Cup or
John Joe shooting from the forty.
Heroes in our own minds until night
Fell, and the ghosts beginning to gather
Around the body on the table,
Made us run in out of the moonlit yard.